Tell Me Why

WHY?

There is Day and Night

Linda Crotta Brennan

Published in the United States of America by Cherry Lake Publishing
Ann Arbor, Michigan
www.cherrylakepublishing.com

Content Adviser: Jack Williams, science writer specializing in weather
Reading Adviser: Marla Conn, ReadAbility, Inc.

Photo Credits: © Pete Pahham/ Shutterstock Images, cover, 1, 5; © Dalton Dingelstad/ Shutterstock
Images, cover, 1, 15; © Digital Media Pro/ Shutterstock Images, cover, 1, 11; © slhy/ Shutterstock Images,
cover, 1, 9; © Alexander Ishchenko/ Shutterstock Images, cover, 1, 7; © pixelparticle/ Shutterstock Images,
cover, 1, 19; © michaeljung/ Shutterstock Images, back cover; © ARZTSAMUI/Shutterstock Images, 5;
© siloto/Shutterstock Images, 7; © Johanna Goodyear/Shutterstock Images, 11; © Toa55/Shutterstock
Images, 13; © Olesya Feketa, Shutterstock Images, 15; © Designua/Shutterstock Images, 17; © Alhovik/
Shutterstock Images, 21

Library of Congress Cataloging-in-Publication Data

Brennan, Linda Crotta, author.
  There is day and night / by Linda Crotta Brennan.
      pages cm. -- (Tell me why)
  Summary: "Offers answers to the most compelling questions about the
rotation of the earth. Age-appropriate explanations and appealing photos.
Additional text features and search tools, including a glossary and an
index, help students locate information and learn new words."-- Provided by
publisher.
  Audience: K to grade 3.
  Includes bibliographical references and index.
  ISBN 978-1-63188-007-0 (hardcover) -- ISBN 978-1-63188-050-6 (pbk.) --
ISBN 978-1-63188-093-3 (pdf) -- ISBN 978-1-63188-136-7 (ebook) 1.
Day--Juvenile literature. 2. Earth (Planet)--Rotation--Juvenile literature.
3. Sun--Juvenile literature. I. Title.

QB633.B74 2015
525.35--dc23

2014005709

Cherry Lake Publishing would like to acknowledge the work of The Partnership for 21st Century Skills.
Please visit www.p21.org for more information.

Printed in the United States of America
Corporate Graphics Inc.

Table of Contents

Getting Dark

Moe set up a racetrack along the sidewalk in front of his apartment. He put on his helmet and hopped on his bike. The track had taken Moe all afternoon to plan.

His dad called him. "It's getting dark. Time to come in!"

Moe frowned. "It gets dark too early."

Dad walked over and patted his back. "Tomorrow will be another day."

Moe put his bike away. "Why do we have day and night, anyway?"

MAKE A GUESS!

What would happen to plants and animals on Earth if we didn't have day and night? Share your ideas with a friend or classmate.

Sunsets often turn the clouds bright colors.

"I wish I could stop the sun from setting," said Moe.

"The sun doesn't move," said Dad. "The earth does." He pointed to Moe's bike. "Your wheel spins. The earth spins, too."

"I don't feel the earth spin," said Moe.

Dad tapped the car. "We have to pick up Mom. Let's do an experiment."

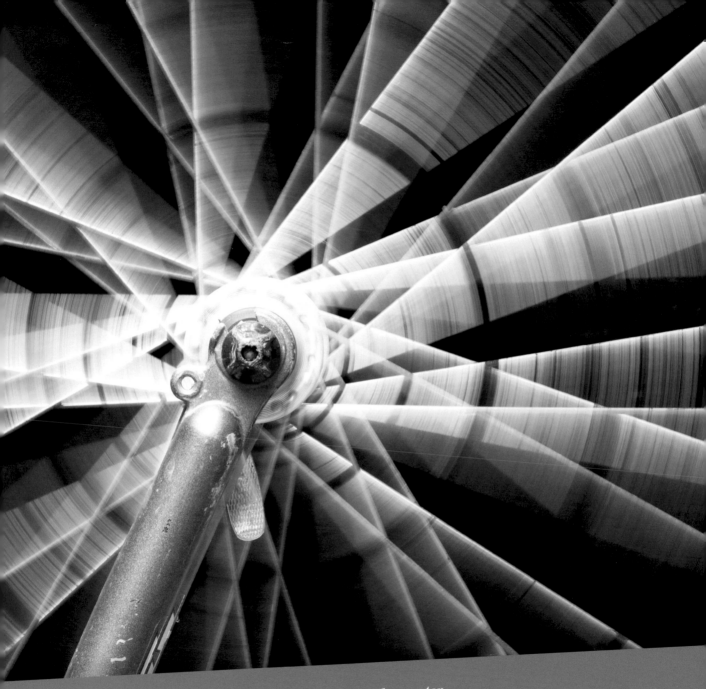

This bike wheel is spinning from a point in the center.

The Earth Spins

Dad drove onto the highway. "We are moving at a steady speed now. Close your eyes." Moe did.

"Do you feel yourself moving?" asked Dad.

"No," said Moe.

Dad sped up.

"Now I do," said Moe.

"That's because I changed speed," said Dad. "We don't feel the earth spin because it moves at a steady speed. We, and everything around us, move with it."

We call this a sunrise, but the sun doesn't actually move.

"How does the earth spinning make day and night?" asked Moe.

Dad parked in front of Mom's office. "As the earth spins, sometimes we face the sun," said Dad. "That's when it's day. Sometimes we face away from the sun. That's when it's night."

Do you know why we say there are 24 hours in a day? Hint: remember that the earth spins.

You can spin a globe to show how the earth spins.

An Experiment

Mom got in the car. She gave Moe a kiss. "How was your day?"

"Fine," said Moe. "I just wish I had more time to play outside after school."

"The days are getting shorter," said Dad.

"How can days get shorter?" asked Moe.

"Let's find our globe when we get home," said Mom. "I'll show you."

Moe found the globe in his room.

The times of sunrises and sunsets change based on the time of year.

"We live here. In the summer, our part of the world is tilted toward the sun. This gives us a longer day and a shorter night," said Mom.

Dad turned on the flashlight.

Mom circled the globe around the light from Dad's flashlight.

"In the winter, our part of the world is tilted away from the sun. This gives us a shorter day and a longer night."

Can you use a globe to find where you live?

Day and night together total 24 hours. At the **equator**, day and night are always the same length. They are both 12 hours long.

At the **South Pole** and **North Pole**, things are very different. The poles have night all winter long and day all summer long. The sun only rises and sets once each season.

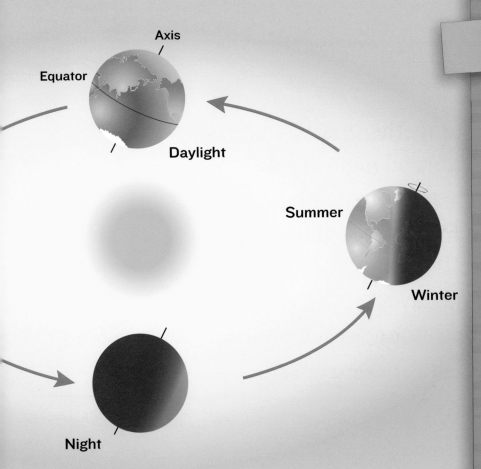

Axis

Equator

Daylight

Summer

Winter

Night

LOOK!

Study this picture. Are you able to explain to a friend or classmate how the earth tilts away from the sun in winter and toward the sun in summer?

*The earth turns around its **axis**.*

Other Planets

Moe looked out the window. "The stars are out. Where do they go during the day?"

Mom smiled. "They are still there. But the sun is too bright for us to see them."

"What about the other planets?" asked Moe. "Do they spin, too?"

"Yes, they do," said Dad.

"But they spin at different speeds," said Mom.

Stars seem to move across the sky as the earth spins.

Moe took out his book about the planets. He flipped through the pages. "Boy, I'm glad I don't live on Jupiter," he said.

"Why?" asked Dad.

"Its day is only 10 hours long," said Moe. "I'd never have enough time to play!"

Sun

Mercury

Venus

Earth

Mars

Jupiter

Saturn

Uranus

Neptune

Earth is the third-closest planet to the sun.

Think About It

What else do you want to know about the earth and sun and planets? Write a list with at least three questions. Then go online, or visit your local library!

Talk with an adult about the difference between the earth spinning and the earth moving around the sun.

What was the most surprising fact you learned from reading this book? Share this book with a friend or classmate and ask him or her the same question. Do your answers match?

Glossary

axis (AK-sis) a line through the center of the earth that it spins around

equator (i-KWAY-tur) an imaginary line around the center of the earth

North Pole (NORTH pohl) the point at the northern end of the earth's axis

South Pole (SOUTH pohl) the point at the southern end of the earth's axis

Find Out More

Books:

Nelson, Robin. *Day and Night*. Minneapolis: Lerner, 2011.

Rau, Dana Meachen. *Day and Night*. Tarrytown, NY: Marshall Cavendish, 2010.

Scott, Korey. *Where Does the Sun Go at Night? An Earth Science Mystery*. Mankato, MN: Capstone 2012.

Web Sites:

Kidcyber—Night and Day
www.kidcyber.com.au/topics/daynight.htm
Visit this page to see an animated video showing the earth rotating on its axis.

StarChild: Question of the Month for March 2001—Why Is There Day and Night?
http://starchild.gsfc.nasa.gov/docs/StarChild/questions/question31.html
NASA's Phil Newman answers this question posed by a young astronomer.

Index

About the Author

Linda Crotta Brennan has a master's degree in education. She spent her life around books, teaching, and working at the library. Now she's a full-time writer who loves learning new things. She lives with her husband and golden retriever. She has three grown daughters and a growing gaggle of grandchildren.